Empath for Beginners

The best guide to nurturing your gift and developing your personality. Improve your relationships with others. Overcome your fears and live to the fullest.

Oliver Bennett

Table of Contents

The following Book is reproduced below with the goal of providing information that is as accurate and reliable as possible. Regardless, purchasing this Book can be seen as consent to the fact that both the publisher and the author of this book are in no way experts on the topics discussed within and that any recommendations or suggestions that are made herein are for entertainment purposes only. Professionals should be consulted as needed prior to undertaking any of the action endorsed herein.

This declaration is deemed fair and valid by both the American Bar Association and the Committee of Publishers Association and is legally binding throughout the United States.

Furthermore, the transmission, duplication, or reproduction of any of the following work including specific information will be considered an illegal act irrespective of if it is done electronically or in print. This extends to creating a secondary or tertiary copy of the work or a recorded copy and is only allowed with the express written consent from the Publisher. All additional right reserved.

The information in the following pages is broadly considered a truthful and accurate account of facts and as such, any inattention, use, or misuse of the information in question by the reader will render any resulting actions solely under their purview. There are no scenarios in which the publisher or the original author of this work can be in any fashion deemed liable for any hardship or damages that may befall them after undertaking information described herein.

Additionally, the information in the following pages is intended only for informational purposes and should thus be thought of as universal. As befitting its nature, it is presented without assurance regarding its prolonged validity or interim quality. Trademarks that are mentioned are done without written consent and can in no way be considered an endorsement from the trademark holder.

EMPATH AND

NARCISSIST

Opposites are drawn toward each other — or so we are told. While this standard can possibly expand your perspectives, individuals who are complete opposites may be drawn together for all an inappropriate reasons.

Narcissists, for instance, are pulled in to individuals they will get the best use from. Often, this implies they seek after and target empaths.

Empaths are something contrary to narcissists. While individuals with narcissistic character issue have no empathy, and flourish with the requirement for appreciation, empaths are profoundly touchy and in line with others' feelings.

Empaths are "passionate wipes," who can assimilate sentiments from others effectively. This makes them exceptionally alluring to narcissists, because they see somebody who will satisfy all their needs in a magnanimous manner.

A 'lethal' fascination bound for debacle

Judith Orloff, a specialist and creator of "The Empath's Survival Guide," revealed to Business Insider this is a harmful fascination which is bound for debacle.

"What narcissists see in empaths is a giving, loving individual who is going to attempt to be given to you and love you and hear you out," she said. "In any case, shockingly empaths are pulled in to narcissists, because from the outset this is about a bogus self. Narcissists present a bogus self, where they can appear to be beguiling and insightful, and in any event, giving, until you don't do things their way, and afterward they get cold, retaining and rebuffing."

When a narcissist is attempting to snare somebody in, they will be loving and mindful, however their cover before long begins to slip. Toward the starting they just observe the great characteristics, and accept the relationship will make them look great. This doesn't last because narcissists are loaded with hatred, and they consider most to be as underneath them. When they begin to see their accomplice's blemishes, they never again admire them, and they begin to reprimand them for not being great.

It can now and then take some time for the real nature to appear, Orloff stated, so she discloses to her customers to never become hopelessly enamored with a narcissist. Be that as it may, this conflicts with an empath's impulses, as they accept they can fix individuals and recuperate anything with sympathy.

"If just they just listened more, if no one but they could give more," said Orloff. "That is simply not the situation with a narcissist. It's so difficult for some empaths to accept that someone simply doesn't have empathy, and that they can't recuperate the other individual with their affection."

Narcissists love dramatization and confusion

Shannon Thomas, a specialist and writer of the book "Recuperating from Hidden Abuse," revealed to Business Insider that empaths buckle down for concordance, though narcissists are hoping to do the inverse. They appreciate disarray, and like to realize they can pull individuals' strings.

Narcissists control empaths by leading them on with discontinuous expectation. They will incorporate commendations and generosity into their conduct, causing their unfortunate casualty to accept that if they carry on in the right way, they will recover the loving individual who they once knew.

"Empathetic individuals tend to comprehend that we're all human, we as a whole have deformities, and they're willing to show restraint toward another person's self-awareness," Thomas said. "Empathetic individuals will be exceptionally patient if a narcissist says 'I truly need to transform, I know I'm not great.' They have these minutes where they kind of concede flaw, however they never really finish or trust it."

This is essentially a strategy narcissists use to reel their accomplice back in. With empaths, it is extremely powerful, because they need to help their accomplice and help them develop. At last, they are simply being abused further.

The empath can shape an injury bond

The push and draw nature of the narcissistic relationship can produce an injury bond between the person in question and the abuser, where it can feel practically difficult to leave the relationship, regardless of how much harm it is doing.

"With empathy comes the capacity and eagerness to take a gander at ourselves and take a gander at our very own flaws, and that gets exploited while the injury bond is going on," Thomas said. "It turns into a cycle for an empath who has been injury fortified because they start taking a gander at themselves, and what do they have to do to change, and what do they have to do different, and what their character defects are. It's the ideal set up, shockingly."

It very well may be difficult to grasp the reality you are in a narcissistic relationship from the outset, yet there are numerous warnings you can pay special mind to as you become more acquainted with one another better. Thomas said to protect yourself from narcissistic maltreatment, you ought to comprehend we are answerable for our very own development, and others are liable for theirs.

"When you meet individuals or are in relationships with them, you must be cautious that you're not doing their work, or needing their development more than they do," she said. "You need to perceive what they really improve."

Additionally, understand that limits are sound for all relationships. For empaths, limits can feel cruel, yet once they know about the quality of saying "no," they can shield themselves from individuals who are hoping to exploit them.

"Empaths don't need to turn out to be hard or remorseless to have the option to be sound," Thomas said. "It's imperative to perceive that not every person should be in our lives. We're going to run over individuals who we understand probably won't be sound for us, and you must approve of releasing them."

What is it about narcissists that is so powerfully alluring?

Like moths attracted to flares, us empaths appear to have an inclination for flying straight into perilous fellowships and soul-sucking relationships that leave us feeling depleted and unhinged. But then, again and again a large number of us fall into a similar snare, often missing the imperative life exercises being displayed.

Pretty much consistently Sol and I get messages asking about the dynamic among empaths and narcissists. Having been scorched by various different kinds of narcissists myself, I realize exactly that it is so natural to fall into the substantial gravitational draw of such individuals. Like dark openings, narcissists consume your feelings, physical wellbeing, and mental stability, significantly controlling and destroying your discernments and sensibilities.

Stirred Empath Book Advertisement picture

Can any anyone explain why empaths and narcissists – two oppositely contradicted kinds of individuals – feel a practically attractive draw towards one another? There are numerous speculations, yet at its core, I accept that it is Life's method for reestablishing harmony.

For instance, how about we inspect your run of the mill empath. Commonly empaths are profoundly minding, merciful individuals. The empath's motivation in life is to help recuperating in others, yet because of their serious affectability, empaths often battle to make sound limits for themselves, yielding to affliction, victimhood, codependency, and ceaseless selflessness. Presently, how about we inspect your average narcissist. Because of different injuries, center injuries and conditionings, narcissists hole up behind a glorified mental self-view which is communicated as being exceptionally enchanting and appealing, yet profoundly cutthroat, indifferent, conceited and coldblooded. Set up empaths and narcissists together? Both interact with their "transformed/invert" selves, and both are compelled to learn, develop and recuperate because of such an encounter (despite the fact that this doesn't generally happen promptly, however through experimentation). Be that as it may, it is significant for empaths to understand that they can never "mend" the narcissists in their lives – any type of recuperating must start inside narcissist's themselves.

Types of Narcissists All Empaths Should Look Out For

Such a large number of books out there talk about "ensuring" yourself from narcissists. Shockingly, this language advances the undermining idea that "others are out to get you." They're definitely not. Individuals act inside the breaking points of their cognizant limit, and in some cases that includes harming others. The more you see yourself as an "injured individual" of narcissists/narcissism, the less proficient you'll be of really owning your own capacity as an empath.

A major piece of owning this individual intensity of yours is figuring out how to identify different sorts of narcissists. The more cognizant you are of them, the more intentionally you'll have the option to carry on and settle on choices in their essence.

Fundamental Types

Strikingly there are really two primary sorts of narcissists:

Defenseless Narcissists (VN's)

These individuals are commonly delicate and will in general be calm or modest essentially. However to camouflage their incessant sentiments of self-hatred and disgracefulness, VN's overcompensate by putting on an affected cover, looking to combine their characters with other admired individuals.

VN's have an unshakeable need to feel exceptional about themselves and have minimal certified respect for the sentiments of others. VN's are principally persuaded by dread of dismissal and deserting, in this manner don't have the ability to authentically love and think about others. Furthermore, VN's utilization enthusiastic control, (for example, disgracing, blame stumbling and gaslighting) to verify compassion and consideration from others. Their lives are fuelled by feelings of inadequacy which often originate from youth abuse.

Immune Narcissists (IN's)

These individuals mirror the conventional picture of the narcissist: that of an exceptionally fearless individual, cold and unempathetic individual. IN's, not normal for VN's, are tough and improperly look for power, brilliance, acknowledgment, and joy. IN's often experience the ill effects of god buildings, trusting themselves to be far better than every other person – and they have a neurotic need to make that known.

The two kinds share comparative characteristics, for example, utilizing others to fuel their narcissistic hallucinations, accusing and condemning, absence of empathy, unfaithfulness and the requirement for power.

Subtypes

Both Vulnerable and Invulnerable Narcissistic character types can be part down into the accompanying (informal) subtypes. Know that a large number of these subtypes can cover with one another:

The Amorous Narcissist

Passionate Narcissists measure their self-esteem and gaudiness by what number of sexual successes they have added to their repertoire.

This sort of individual is known for utilizing his/her fascinate to entrap others with blandishment and gifts, however then rapidly discarding them once they become "exhausting" and when they have met the narcissists needs (often sexual or picture/status orientated).

Desirous Narcissists are a definitive relationship extortionists, "gold diggers" and heart-breakers. From the start, they show up exceptionally appealing, charming and friendly, yet underneath they are just out to please and satisfy their very own needs and wants.

The Compensatory Narcissist

Headed to make up for past injuries, Compensatory Narcissists love making overwhelming fantasies of themselves and their accomplishments. So as to recover force and authority over their lives, this kind of narcissist for the most part chases out genuinely powerless individuals who will fill in as the crowd to their manufactured stage acts. As a general rule, this sort of narcissist is amazingly touchy to analysis and will habitually pay special mind to negative self-coordinated signals from others. Psychological mistreatment and control is a typical strategy for control utilized by this sort.

The Elitist Narcissist

This type of individual successfully move to the "top," win and totally command others. Elitist narcissists are persuaded that they are superior to every other person often because of their accomplishments or foundations (or just the way that they were brought into the world that way) and in this manner merit exceptional treatment. Their feeling of privilege seeps into each everyday issue, from work to the family condition. Harboring a seriously swelled conscience, Elitist narcissists are gifted self-advertisers, braggers, and one-uppers. They have a merciless should be simply the "best" and demonstrate to be mentally prevalent constantly and no matter what.

The Malignant Narcissist

The conduct of dangerous narcissists often covers with that of mental cases and those with solitary character issue. Dangerous narcissists often have no respect or enthusiasm for moral versus corrupt conduct and don't feel regret for their activities. This subgroup is portrayed by a pompous and expanded feeling of self-esteem that savors the experience of "outmaneuvering" others. This kind of narcissist can often be found in detainment facilities, groups, and medication restoration focuses, albeit many figure out how to cross paths with the law.

Phases of Relationship Between An Empath and A Narcissist

1 The empath gets pulled in to a narcissist. Their relationship begins. Empath adores profoundly and genuinely. They feel genuinely satisfied despite the fact that the narcissist assumes no job to build up a more grounded bond.

The empath feels fulfilled and thinks their adoration is responded just by being around the narcissist.

2 The empath gets the bogus thought that they have at last met the sort of affection that individuals don't discover even once. Narcissist avows this by making a hallucination that leads the empath to accept that what they have is uncommon. The empath feels a profound bond that is practically difficult to break free.

3 Sometimes apparently the narcissist needs this relationship as much as the empath. All things considered, what they need is somebody who contributes their time, vitality and love and is in their unlimited authority.

4 As the time will pass, the narcissist will make the empath feel frail, unconfident, and dispossessed of the capacities to do even the straightforward things. The narcissist will never dispatch an open assault, yet use proclamations like "would prefer not to hurt you yet... " to call attention to some weakness.

They will attempt to assume control over anything which symbolizes control, for example, dealing with bills or settling on choices about buys. The empathy will be looked downward on for their inclinations and numerous such things that structure their character. Steadily, the empath begins to accept that they are less competent and they "need" somebody like the individual in their life. They get the thought nobody would need them.

5 For an empath, this relationship will be everything as they are the ones who are enamored. Out of adoration, they would consistently need to relieve and cheer the narcissist, converse with them, help them and do whatever it makes them feel better. The narcissists venture themselves as the casualty of their past, their relationships, and the conditions. The empaths are providers; they attempt to compensate for all the tragic things that have ever happened to the narcissist.

6 The empath has a decent and a reasonable heart and can't envision the profound and uncertain injuries of the narcissist are not equivalent to their own. Recuperating those injuries is different from their own.

7 The relationship is about the narcissist. The empath understands this gradually, and an opportunity arrives when they feel hesitant to talk or battle for their needs and wants. In their endeavor to satisfy they would prefer not to voice their actual needs. They would prefer to be agreeable than give any motivation to be disdained. Be that as it may, furtively they are troubled.

8 The more dedication, love, care, love, and exertion the empath places into the relationship, the narcissist feels totally in charge of the relationship. The empath actually moves to the tune of the narcissist. For whatever length of time that the empath keeps on pacifying the narcissist, it's difficult to recognize any issue in the relationship. The issue happens when the empath at long last arrives at the limit.

9 Finally, the empath raises a voice because they can never again stay aware of the smothering methods for the narcissist. For quite a while their passionate needs stay unfulfilled. This happens because from the earliest starting point of the relationship they have accepted their accomplice's enthusiastic needs are the only thing that is in any way important. When they at last comprehend their prosperity additionally matters, and stand up, they appear to be narrow minded. The narcissist doesn't care for it.

10 The narcissist is a consideration searcher. They get fulfillment when individuals whine around them. Their needs can never be met, they can never be fulfilled. They may move to different accomplices, open another business, travel far and wide, engage in new innovative interests, et cetera, however they will never be glad. The empath doesn't know about this reality.

11 When the empath at long last blasts out something like "My emotions likewise matter," the narcissist rushes to call the empath "insane". They bring them over-sensational and their interests unwarranted. This sort of pretentious conduct is the strategies utilized by them to deal with the empath's brain.

12 The empath gets confounded. Why they have dispensed such conduct, is outside their ability to grasp. They start accusing themselves and miracle if they are at all deserving of being adored by anybody by any means.

13 At this point, the empath can't comprehend that they are simply being controlled. Their accomplice has bowed everything around them to make a contorted perspective on the conditions. There can be anything around them to tell them reality that they are the person who is "correct" and it's their accomplice who is hugely "wrong" and evil.

14 The empath will attempt to speak with the narcissist in all honesty. The narcissist will, in any case, justify their conduct and pass the fault.

15 It is ordinary to feel lost, befuddled and hurt. In any case, in spite of all the heart-break, the empath should be quiet and do some self-assessment to make sense of how they turned out to be so exposed. This is the way they will begin changing.

16 The empath will realize that they are essentially healers. They have the internal solidarity to help other people in the correct manners, now and then as an obligation and here and there when life carries them to such circumstances.

17 The empath needs to understand the harsh truth that not every person merits their adoration, care, and friendship. Not every person who appears to be upset and miserable is uncovering their actual self. There are a few people who have vile intentions and have a totally different standpoint towards relationships and individuals than they do. Not every person they experience passionate feelings for can be trusted so rapidly.

18 In this circumstance, the empath must understand that they also are in a terrible circumstance something of which the narcissist in their life consistently discussed. Be that as it may, for their situation, it would be different. They would try positive endeavors and mend themselves. The narcissist won't.

19 For empath this will be a difficult arousing. They will gain from the experience to push forward.

20 The narcissist will proceed as though nothing occurred and they are totally guiltless. They won't recollect for a minute that somebody cherished them so profoundly and seriously. They won't recall the incredible bond they once had with somebody and simply proceed onward to discover it elsewhere. An opportunity will come when they will realize they can neither interface with themselves nor with others.

21 The narcissist will proceed onward. In time they will discover another injured individual.

22 The empath will be more grounded, more astute and be increasingly careful about who they time, warmth and love.

The dangerous truth behind this perplexing matching.

For what reason are empaths and narcissists pulled in to one another? The matching of these two character attributes can be a perilous and dangerous relationship, and here's the reason.

A narcissist is an individual who is self-assimilated and comes up short on the capacity to empathize with others.

Particularly in the present day and age with the ascent of web based life and realism, everybody can be somewhat narcissistic to a certain extent. It is a character characteristic that exists on a continuum. In any case, on the out and out clinical level, you can have a Narcissistic Personality Disorder, which is a dysfunctional behavior that seriously weakens sound working. A narcissist will in general utilize others as a way to end to satisfy their own needs without minding how the other individual is influenced and to verify their place on focal point of the audience.

An empath, then again, has a remarkable inverse issue. They think that its simple to identify with other's sentiments, to such an extent truth be told, that they genuinely feel what others feel.

They often will think about others to the detriment of dealing with themselves. "For empaths ... we really feel others' feelings, vitality, and physical indications in our own bodies, without the standard protections that a great many people have," says Dr. Judith Orloff, creator of The Empath's Survival Guide.

It is essential to take note of that while Narcissistic Personality Disorder — normally known as NPD — is a mental ailment that must be analyzed by a qualified and profoundly experienced psychological wellness proficient, numerous individuals have prevailing narcissistic character characteristics. In this book, we utilize the pronouns "he" to show the individual with narcissistic character attributes and "she" for the empath and those with empathatic characteristics — notwithstanding, remember this is for simplicities purpose and females can be narcissists similarly as guys can be empaths.

Presently you may be asking: Why on the planet would two such disparate people even locate each other pulled in any case?

This is an instance of opposites are drawn toward each other. Both have what the other individual needs a when they meet up, it makes for a harmful fascination.

The empath needs somebody that they can think about and the narcissist can detect this and utilize the empath by controlling her for his own motivations. Narcissists can be charming and can even fake love and care when it will get them what they need. Fundamentally, a narcissist is an injured person. In some cases the turmoil originates from early youth encounters if they had not gotten enough love and consideration. They will along these lines start to pine for the consideration and approval from others yet will be not able give real love consequently.

The empath, being the overseers that they are, can detect this fundamental injury and will need to do all that they can support their accomplice. What they may not see is that the narcissist is a taker that will benefit from the empath like a vitality vampire.

An empath surprisingly, being so instinctive, can often detect that their accomplice is a narcissist yet it isn't so basic.

Generally an empath can detect in some way or another that their accomplice isn't generally equipped for loving them really. Be that as it may, much the same as any harsh relationship, it tends to be difficult to escape the cycle of fascination and devastation. Whenever she gets injured, she will end up detached because the narcissist is plainly not one that will be able to comfort her.

Moreover, he will be truly adept at shifting fault for offenses from himself, further defrauding his accomplice.

Regardless of how awful it gets, the empath will hang on because she imagines that she can mend him. She wouldn't like to disregard him, a man with no social aptitudes like her, because what will happen to him?

It's urgent for the empath to understand that the narcissist is injured to the final turning point. They just don't have the natural capacity to empathize. She should escape the relationship before the further maltreatment wears her confidence and vitality out further. It won't beat that, it will just deteriorate.

What's more, the narcissist, being unequipped for empathy, won't be the one with the sense to put a conclusion to the injurious relationship.

It is the duty of the empath to break out of the segregation, look for outside help, and desert the relationship.

The most effective method to Leave A Narcissist

You don't need to stay.

When you're in a relationship with a narcissist, they can make you begin to look all starry eyed at them so hard that it feels like you're surrendering a piece of your heart to leave them.

Furthermore, what a narcissist does toward the finish of a relationship can be dubious, as they'll utilize each control procedure in the book to get you to remain in a genuinely oppressive relationship with them.

Superficially, narcissists can appear to be enchanting, canny, mindful — realizing how to allure and draw their way again into your life. Be that as it may, when they reel you back, they return to their boastful selves.

That is the reason parting ways with a narcissist is no simple accomplishment.

Their maxim will consistently be "Me first!"

Everything's about them. They have a bombastic feeling of vainglory and qualification, long for reverence and consideration.

They can likewise be profoundly instinctive, however utilize their instinct for personal responsibility and control, some of the time intensifying to the degree of narcissistic maltreatment.

Narcissists are so perilous because they need empathy and have a constrained limit with regards to genuine love.

Tragically, their hearts either haven't created or have been closed down, potentially because of early mental injury, for example, being raised by narcissistic guardians, a devastating impediment both genuinely and profoundly. Hard as it might be to appreciate, these individuals have little understanding into their activities, nor do they lament them.

To see whether you've been in a relationship with a narcissist, ask yourself the accompanying inquiries:

Does the individual go about as though life spins around him?

Do I need to praise him to stand out enough to be noticed or endorsement?

Does he always control the discussion back to himself?

Does he make light of my sentiments or interests?

If I deviate, does he become cold or retaining?

If you answer "yes" to a couple of inquiries, it's feasible you're managing a narcissist. Reacting "yes" to at least three inquiries proposes that a narcissist is damaging your passionate opportunity, possibly to the point of misuse.

Narcissists are hard nuts to pop open.

With these patients, all the better I can do is line up with their positive perspectives and spotlight on practices that they concur aren't working. In any case, regardless of whether one needs to change, progress is constrained, with small gains.

My expert guidance: Don't experience passionate feelings for a narcissist or engage dreams they're fit for the give and take important for closeness. In such relationships, you'll generally be sincerely alone somewhat.

If you have a retention narcissist mate, be careful with attempting to win the supporting you never got from your folks; it won't occur. Additionally, don't hope to have your affectability respected. These individuals harsh love with every one of the loops you should hop through to satisfy them.

If you're considering saying a final farewell to a narcissist or attempting to make sense of what a narcissist does toward the finish of a relationship that keeps you with them, utilize these strategies to recover your capacity.

1. Try not to succumb to their controls.

They will make every effort imaginable to get you back, so be readied. Narcissists are truly persuading. When you are prepared to leave, adhere to your feelings and proceed onward to an increasingly positive future loaded up with genuine love.

2. Set cutoff points and limits.

Since narcissists have no empathy, nor can they truly cherish, so you should leave them immediately and bear the torment. Set points of confinement and state "no" to them. Then accumulate your entire existence and continue strolling into the obscure towards something better.

3. Concentrate on what's to come.

When segregated from a narcissist, it is critical that you concentrate all your positive vitality and considerations on doing beneficial things for yourself and the world. Try not to let your psyche meander to the past or to what he is doing.

4. Be thoughtful to yourself.

Fortune yourself. Be thoughtful to yourself and realize that you merit a loving relationship with somebody who can respond that adoration.

My view on life is that each individual we meet en route, loving or not, is intended to enable us to develop.

Try not to whip yourself for engaging with a narcissist.

In any case, it would be ideal if you take in what you can from it, including defining solid limits and saying "no" to manhandle, so you don't rehash this exercise.

It is genuinely liberating to recuperate any fascination in injurious individuals so you can have all the more genuine romance in your life.

If You Have These 30 Traits, Consider Yourself An Empath

You're exceptional.

Empaths are genuinely associated with others. They can truly add something extra to circumstances and tune in inside and out. Not every person has the character characteristics that empaths are sufficiently fortunate to have.

Without a doubt, it might appear to be a weight from the start because they feel things so profoundly. Feelings can run high and some of the time cause some internal nerves and surliness. In any case, every one of those emotions are utilized as more noteworthy bits of knowledge into life. They can see the world differently than others. That is extraordinary.

You or somebody you know might be an empath. If you are, congrats! You will perpetually be the individual that numerous individuals hurry to for guidance, reassuring, and only a benevolent nearness. That is an astonishing capacity to have.

See whether you or anybody you know have any of the qualities that are signs you're an empath!

1. Knowing

Empaths have a profound feeling of realizing that is resolute and undeniable which accompanies pinpoint exactness in its depiction. They are equipped for perusing others without evident prompts and can depict what's truly going on underneath the surface. They know if somebody is being untrustworthy or not talking their certainties. The more adjusted they are to their empathy the more grounded and progressively visit the knowing and perusing capacities will be.

2. Successful Listeners And Communicators

A characteristic capacity to tune in with every one of their faculties intensely adjusted enabling the individual to feel just as they are being heard and comprehended.

They can naturally direct a discussion with genuine sympathy empowering even the most held individual to react and express their most profound and even most excruciating considerations and sentiments they wouldn't usually share.

In most case, it is completed in an implicit certainty and trust, yet if a circumstance conceivably calls for outside mediation (for example self-hurt) they will weigh up the need to act to the greatest advantage of that individual, not self, regardless of whether it implies gambling continuous relations.

3. Overpowered In Public Places

Shopping centers, general stores or arenas where masses of individuals accumulate can be overpowering and even lead to freeze assaults or nervousness because of the horde of feelings being detected and until this is contained and reasonable they will avoid being in said environment.

4. Feeling Others Emotions Pains, Illnesses And Stresses

Due to increased sensitivities to passionate and physical vitality, it is a typical event to accept the feelings and so forth of others and not understand they are doing as such. Legitimately reflecting it as if it was their own.

It can make it difficult to recognize what is having a place with self or another and life can turn out to be amazingly overpowering. Mindfulness brings a more noteworthy level of control and the capacity to decide whose feelings and so forth are whose and not become involved with it.

5. Emotional episodes, Unpredictable And Needy

They can encounter outrageous highs and lows which makes them eccentric in conduct under the most favorable circumstances. Brief they can be cheerful and the following moment miserable and pulled back which isn't generally the aftereffect of how they really feel yet what they have gotten in others, this can be befuddling not to mention discouraging.

They can likewise be requesting of consideration, be it for valid justifications or not. If they believe they are not being heard they will carry on and appear to be destitute, even narcissistic, despite the fact that they would genuinely address and restrict the last mentioned. Because one may have solid empathy sooner or later in time doesn't mean they are not much the same as being so overpowered with it that they fall intensely towards narcissism.

6. Delicate to TV, Radio, and Movies And Real Life Chaos

Savagery, cold-bloodedness, stunning scenes of physical or enthusiastic torment or misuse can bring an empath to tears. They may even feel physically poorly, confused and battle to grasp such goes about as being justified. One sure method for managing this is to kill the TV or radio or disassociating yourself from the tumult.

7. Inclined To Illness, Disease And Physical Pain

Because of the invasion of passionate vitality, they are excessively delicate as well and as a rule, they don't have the foggiest idea how to manage this can get hazardous and manifest into fluctuating types of ailments or malady.

It is essential to find out about passionate vitality, recognize its root and apply the apparatuses that will enable the individual to push ahead with adjusted wellbeing. Existing ailments and illness can possibly be let go unequivocally in doing as such.

8. Attractive Pull Of Trust

Others, including outsiders, are attracted to an empath like a magnet and think that it's simple to communicate and impact them on a profound and important level; they will often feel like they have known each other for a long time despite the fact that they may have quite recently met.

Individuals have this intrinsic feeling of trust and feel great and loose in their quality yet are cognizant they would not regularly feel along these lines.

9. Steady Fatigue

They are attracted to helping other people and in doing so take on too much to by and by adapt to both inwardly, rationally, physically and profoundly and will encounter consistent weakness. They may need to take every day catnaps or withdraws just to recharge their vitality and feel rejuvenated.

10. Addictive Behavior

Can be brought about by needing to escape from what they are barraged with or a urgent need to feel associated.

Their uplifted sensitivities more than often don't accompany an attention to how to manage it, (the energies they get on like wipes) not to mention what's going on and they will receive addictive inclinations to overwhelm, numb and occupy them, for example, drinking, smoking, consuming medications, gorging to betting and so on.

Tragically for a few, in doing as such (for example ingesting medications) it can elevate their sensitivities considerably more and make more prominent issues.

11. Mending, Holistic Health, And Wellness

Regardless of whether it is a vocation as an attendant, specialist, physiotherapist, neurosurgeon, analyst or back rub advisor, homeopath, naturopath, Chinese prescription expert and social laborers or a veterinarian, the individuals who have solid empathy since early on are often attracted to these fields because of a destroy to mending individuals and additionally creatures.

Severe and long haul instruction and work conventions, be that as it may, is known to stifle ones intrinsic empathy and surprisingly hinder them from what attracted them to the field the primary spot. Once in the field, there is an incredible should know about one's empathy and not become overpowered in taking on others vitality as it can turn into an impetus in wearing out and leaving through and through.

12. Interest And Seekers Of The Truth

Driven by interest to comprehend the complexities of life and an extraordinary want to look for reality and question quite a bit of everything until they feel a reverberation to some random answer, if it doesn't agree with them their interest will develop and they will keep on looking for answers regardless of whether it takes a lifetime.

13. Interests In Spirituality And Metaphysical

They can be attracted to the unexplainable, paranormal, mysticism and have a profound feeling of otherworldliness (not really religion despite the fact that they may lean towards such so as to discover a feeling of having a place). They will fiddle with numerous regions until they discover their specialty and they will effectively seek after it all through their lifetime.

14. Social And Indigenous

They are attracted to antiquated societies that hold fast to since quite a while ago held customs shrouded in all inclusive laws as they typify intrinsic rationale, good judgment and useful uncomplicated manners by which to do all way of things. They will often shake their head in dismay when others do and act in a manner that restricts all inclusive laws.

15. Tribal Lineage — Who Am I?

Since early on, they are the youngster that tunes in to the narratives of old that are passed down all through the ages. They have a veritable enthusiasm for needing to know where they originated from and who their precursors were and what they did in their lifetime and will grow up to be attendants of the family tree and have an assortment of photograph collections and treasures. Feeling a feeling of connectedness holds extraordinary significance and as they get familiar with this, they thus will be the one to give this information to their kids.

In spite of the fact that they hush up achievers who want to do the hard yards off camera they will often be found in places of administration because of their capacity to be engaged, sorted out and steady, snappy reasoning and equipped for rousing and persuading others with magnificent balance.

They are progressively agreeable in giving earnest acclaim to others as opposed to tolerating it and are often found intervening to keep up a parity of congruity.

17. Inventive Talents

An extraordinary love for communicating their innovativeness as specialists, artists, vocalists, artists, performing craftsmen, acting, writers, and fashioners and so forth. They love to recount to a story and can enthrall a group of people through a striking creative mind and a straightforwardness wherein they can take you legitimately into the image as if you were really encountering it firsthand.

18. Love Of Nature And Animals

Slanted to have a pet as they love to give and get unqualified love that originates from hounds, felines, hares and so forth and are often promoters or supporters in the counteractive action of pitilessness to creatures.

They appreciate being outside, among the backwoods or high in the mountains and are content being associated with the land and will often escape from the bustling scene to restore their faculties.

19. Purifying Water

Be it swimming in the ocean, drifting in the pool, strolling in the downpour, a long absorb the tub or a hot shower to rinse and wash away the difficulties of the day, they sense the mending properties of water and reconnection to the belly for the wellbeing and solace it held can be recovered right then and there.

20. Requirement For Solitude

Despite the fact that they can be truly agreeable, they likewise prefer to escape from the rushing about and are content with their very own organization getting a charge out of the peacefulness that accompanies being in a calm space perusing a book, viewing a motion picture, drawing an image, seeking after a diversion they love to simply unwinding. They will show this propensity from adolescence and all through life.

21. Fatigue, Distracted, And Daydreaming

A should be invigorated and centered around some venture and will give all their vitality to some random errand whether it is at school, work or home life. If the undertaking neglects to invigorate their faculties they become exhausted, occupied and will either start to squirm, doodle or be off in their brains wandering off in fantasy land.

22. Experience Seekers, Travel And Spontaneous

Appreciate immediacy in their life by investigating all that life brings to the table and will search out experiences, travel to faraway places or find agreeable exercises close by.

They appreciate being free-energetic, leaving the imperatives of the world behind them and if they don't get the chance to do this as often as they might want will turn out to be very fretful and disturbed.

23. Mess, Energy, And Flow

An attention to vitality falls into place without any issues and they will feel weighted somewhere near mess and bedlam, despite the fact that they may gather things everything has a put in and request and they will always mess clearing to permit the equalization of vitality (stream) in their condition. They have a capacity to put furniture or even plant cultivates such that vitality streams in and around everything.

24. Rule Breakers

Schedule, redundancy, and rules can get commonplace for the imaginative empath who consistently look for manners by which to express their loves, the things they appreciate in life. If they are told they can't accomplish something, sensibly speaking they will discover a way that they can as the ability to challenge themselves goes connected at the hip with being unconstrained.

25. Eagerness And Appreciation Of Life

Overflowing with vitality and a gratefulness towards life and living it as completely as they can is loaded up with energy. In any case, the drawback is they can apply so a lot of vitality that they will wear out and need to set aside some effort to recover and when they do they will ricochet back and give themselves completely.

They don't do anything in equal parts; it's win or bust and they will in general feel frustrated if others around them don't have a similar vitality as they do.

26. Helpful people, Peacemakers, And Mediators

Struggle is incredibly agitating in any case if it is with family, companions, partners or even total outsiders or if it is immediate or roundabout, locally or universally and will voice their sentiments towards such. They will attempt to locate a serene goals regardless of whether it implies being a middle person.

They have an adoration and regard surprisingly and societies and intensely restrict wars, political agitation, savagery, prejudice, contempt and dissidence as they accept profoundly that we would all be able to live respectively in concordance and will advocate this somehow, if not by being critical to the foundation of compassionate associations or on the side of.

27. Delicate To Antiques, Vintage Or Second-hand

Holding books, for example, rings, gems, apparel, trimmings or contacting entryway handles to old structures, entering authentic homes and so on can bring through distinctive and precise records of the owner(s) history and life encounters.

This can be very overwhelming and off-putting to those delicate to getting energies, though the individuals who are increasingly mindful and in charge of their empathy will feel calm, and be attracted to such.

28. Clear Dreamers

The fantasy domain isn't only an aimless spot where one goes when they are sleeping. An empath often has striking dreams from an exceptionally youthful age and all through and will have clear dreams where they are wakeful in their fantasies and have a capacity to control certain perspectives by resolved idea alone and are fit for portraying in realistic detail the fantasy content.

They likewise want to translate the fantasy realizing that it has direct significance to their physically wakeful life and in doing so can discover answers to control them well. It isn't surprising for an empath to sooner or later in time in their lives to have encountered and Out of Body Experience or Astral Travel, be it willfully or not.

29. Sweethearts Not Fighters

Empaths love to cherish others and be adored in kind and will look for significant relationships all through their whole lives, however they are not constantly capable at self-esteem as they are slanted to give of themselves openly to other people and can grow up intuition (by what they gain from society) that it is narrow minded to adore thine self and that that is narcissistic in conduct.

They don't prefer to be up to speed in battles be it verbal or physical as correspondence comes effectively to them, be that as it may, they won't be detached either however they will focus on a tranquil goals as fast as could be expected under the circumstances. They will get amazingly disappointed if the other individual isn't happy to determine the contention completely as they don't see the rationale in hauling things on.

30. Visionaries, Entrepreneurial And Problem Solvers

Exceptional visionaries mixed with their bold love of life streak and energy they will fiddle with numerous endeavors and business openings and discover manners by which to grow their latent capacity, feed their imaginative personalities and do the things they love to do.

They have this instinctual realizing they are fit for accomplishing more prominent things and will continually consider new ideas and push through all limits, (often against the chances) with centered and hound decided vitality. Where there is an issue, their promptly lies an answer and they won't stop until they think that its regardless of whether that implies imagining it themselves!

It is critical to take note of that a great many people experience differing degrees of empathy, in any case, if you can say yes to most, if not the entirety of the above you unquestionably are an empathy.

HOW TO RECOVER AND HEAL FROM NARCISSISTIC ABUSE

"Try not to censure a jokester for acting like a comedian. Wonder why you prop up to the carnival."
~Unknown

When I originally experienced narcissistic maltreatment as a grown-up, it was a when the expression "narcissistic maltreatment" was not all that knew about or comprehended.

I had met an attractive, wise, magnetic, and beguiling man, and as is regular in oppressive relationships, had been totally overpowered by the power and 'love'-over-burden of the beginning times.

Before I could pause, however, the criticizing began, thus did the warmed contentions, the desire, the cutting contact, and vanishing for quite a long time—instantly pursued by sensational make-ups, statements of regret, gifts, and guarantees.

Thus had started the enthusiastic thrill ride that is dating a narcissist.

Numerous months after the fact, I wound up turning into a different individual. I was pushed, restless, distrustful, progressively confined, and crotchety. I was completely lost and felt like no one comprehended. Companions couldn't comprehend why we couldn't simply end things. We were snared in a dangerous bond.

Even under the least favorable conditions focuses being trapped in a poisonous relationship feels completely angering. Following quite a while of relationship highs and lows, of it being on and off, the gaslighting, allegations, and coercive control, I sincerely started to trust I was losing my psyche.

I was adhered attempting to comprehend my experience, and the consistent piece of my psyche was frantically looking for answers to such huge numbers of inquiries:

For what reason did he cheat?

What was so amiss with me?

For what reason did he lie?

What were lies and what was reality?

Was any of it genuine?

Did he ever truly express the words he said?

—

Is it safe to say that he was even equipped for affection?

How could things have been different?

What else could or would it be a good idea for me to have done?

These are a portion of similar inquiries I hear my customers pose to now when they come to me for help in recuperating from narcissistic maltreatment.

The Journey of Healing

My very own recuperation began one especially unglued night. I was unimaginably disturbed and urgent to understand what was happening. Looking through on the web, I happened to run over data about sociopaths and narcissists and this specific sort of mental maltreatment.

This was an essential minute. I had never heard anyone utilize the expression "narcissistic maltreatment," and around then (this was numerous years prior), there was not really any data around about it. However, I knew, the minute I read this, this was it. It shifted my entire viewpoint. It was stunning, confounding, albeit by and large, a mind boggling alleviation. I understood this was a 'thing' and that just because, others comprehended. All the more significantly, there was an exit plan.

Perusing increasingly about mental maltreatment, I landed at my first key point in mending:

I Realized It's Not Me—I'm Not Crazy!

Lethal relationships will leave you having an inclination that you are distraught. Often harsh accomplices will strengthen this by never assuming liability and continually letting you know in different manners that it is your deficiency or your issues.

My narcissistic accomplice would reprimand and undermine me in a wide range of odd and unobtrusive ways, including decisions or 'recommendations.' He would often convey in manners that would leave me questioning or addressing myself. Just like the intensity of being with a narcissist, at the time, I was anxious to please and intrigue.

If I at any point pulled him up on any of the reactions, he blamed me for being pessimistic, revealed to me he was attempting to help my self-improvement, that I was being touchy, distrustful, that I was over-responding, or that I had issues. This sort of maltreatment in itself is incensing. I understood that all of what I had been feeling was in itself the indications of being in a genuinely harsh relationship.

I was not and am not frantic, yet I was in a distraught relationship. I found as I cut contact and expelled myself from the lethal powerful that my feeling of mental soundness swiftly returned. This is something that numerous sufferers I work with now likewise experience. You are not insane, however if you are in an injurious relationship, you are in a relationship dynamic that will leave you having an inclination that you are.

Relinquishing the Need to Understand and Know

It's our mind's regular propensity to need to comprehend our experience; in any case, with narcissism and narcissistic conduct, there is no sense. You can't have any significant bearing rationale to silly activities. I made a great deal of misery for myself in the early piece of my recuperation by urgently sticking onto the dream that I by one way or another could see all the what's and whys.

Having the option to relinquish this need to know is a major advance in recuperation. This was difficult at the time, yet I dealt with this by rehearsing care and figuring out how to perceive when my musings or consideration would drift to the narcissist or on attempting to work out the appropriate responses or comprehend the non-existent rationale.

As I got mindful of my considerations drifting to such a vain errand, I would then attempt to tune into my emotions at that time and ask myself "How am I feeling at this moment?"

I'd rationally name the feeling and any physical vibes that accompanied it.

Then, knowing all the more obviously how I was feeling (tragic, furious, and so on.) I would ask myself "What do I need? What would i be able to accomplish for myself right now that is a loving and steady activity?"

At times this is enable myself to cry, punch a cushion, connect with a companion, or proceed to get myself something pleasant—to rehearse self-care. It was a bit by bit procedure to discover manners by which I could tenderly feel my emotions and take care of my own needs. This likewise incorporated the emotions I had about not having answers and tolerating that perhaps I never will. You can tenderly give up with this pull together and self-care. Settle on a decision about what might be destructive of accommodating to your recuperating and recuperation.

Thinking about My Own Narcissism

I chuckle since my separation kept going longer than the genuine relationship! The dangerous dynamic was addictive and extremely difficult to relinquish from the two sides.

An empath will mind, excuse, comprehend, and put a narcissist's needs before their own. A narcissist will pine for the consideration, contact, and force. It turns into a move.

Narcissists will in general have a disrupted connection style. Relationships will be push and pull, on and off, here and there. Being in a relationship with a narcissist is a ton like being on an enthusiastic thrill ride. It's invigorating and depleting, however if you remain on, going all around for a considerable length of time you will become ill!

Because of the connection style, the minute a narcissist detects you are pulling ceaselessly, they will intuitively expect to pull you back in once more, tossing a wide range of trap so as to snare you back.

I was snared back over and over by broken guarantees and needing to accept the dream of how things could be.

I was additionally snared by accepting that some way or another, I could be the one to transform him, to make him see, to assist him with loving and feel cherished, to make things different, to assist him with being the individual I trusted and accepted he could be.

Believe it or not, I needed to be the one to catch and hold his consideration and intrigue. In any case, such is the requests of narcissistic stock that it's outlandish that can ever be one individual for eternity.

In all honesty, I needed to perceive the narcissism in this. To see the narcissistic dream in my thought regarding some way or another having some supernatural forces to assist him with recuperating and change. I can't. Actually, no one can.

A narcissist's mending and activities are their obligation just—no one else's.

Accepting in some way or another you can be 'the one' to change a narcissist is narcissistic somewhat in itself. This doesn't mean someone who has this expectation has narcissistic character issue! It's only useful to perceive the poorly put expectation and dream.

Narcissism is one of the most difficult clinical introductions for profoundly experienced masters to treat. You don't have the capacity or capacity to change or support an abuser. More to the point, for what reason would you need to?

Relinquish Fantasy Thinking and Ground Yourself in Reality

Numerous individuals who've encountered narcissistic maltreatment gotten caught in tricky dream. Dream believing is sticking onto the expectation of how you accept things could be, not how they really are.

One of the most confounding things I encountered when in a relationship with a narcissist was recognizing the difference among dream and reality. With this there can be an inconsistency among body and psyche. For instance, my ex always revealed to me that he was being steady. In any case, I didn't feel bolstered.

Like in numerous harsh relationships, the words and the activities don't coordinate. It's not possible for anyone to truly mean the words "I love you" and be vicious, basic, or damaging simultaneously.

In recuperation, it is fundamental to recognize the expectation and dream of how things could be and the truth of how things really are. I often hear individuals portray the aching for things to be as were they "to start with."

The beginning of an oppressive relationship can be unimaginably exceptional and amazing. This is the time the controller will 'love-bomb' and it can feel elating, sentimental, amazing, and exceptionally addictive.

Power isn't equivalent to closeness however. Genuine closeness requires some investment and is adjusted. Force can give you a high that you keep on longing for.

If you speculate you are in an unfortunate relationship, it's imperative to take a genuine and target stock of the present reality, not your optimal of how things were or could be. At the present time, how protected and secure do you feel? At present, what are the activities of your accomplice or ex?

It very well may be useful to take pen to paper and rundown the present practices or conditions to help recapture some progressively sensible point of view. Maybe asking companions or family their view as well.

Assume liability

Something I feel generally thankful from my experience of narcissistic maltreatment is that I truly needed to figure out how to assume total liability for myself. I needed to turn out to be completely answerable for myself and my activities; my recuperation, my endeavors, my self-care, my accounts, my wellbeing, my prosperity, my life... everything.

Something I see numerous individuals do while in a poisonous relationship, and in any event, following the finish of one, is to get stayed with concentrating their endeavors and considerations on the narcissist. Over-worrying about what they are presently doing, or not doing, or as yet attempting to get them to see things another way, or waiting for a statement of regret from them, or trusting they will change or satisfy every one of their guarantees, etc.

A specific snare I often catch wind of in my work presently is the oppressive accomplice dangling a 'carrot on a stick' when their accomplice endeavors to cut off the association. This can be exceptionally damaging as they step up the guarantees of furnishing you with whatever it is they realize you wish for; be it legitimate responsibility, a family, a protected home circumstance, money related buys, or more.

I have genuinely yet to hear a record of when any of these guarantees have been respected. Rather, accomplices are left squandering months and years, even decades, hanging on the dream and expectation that an accomplice will give them what they need.

I believe it's essential to perceive the greater point of view. If there are things you need in life, then you assume total liability for getting them going.

Keep in mind, an excess of spotlight on the narcissist is a major piece of the issue in any case!

Mending accompanies restoring your concentration to yourself, recognizing your very own sentiments and passionate experience, perceiving your own needs and needs, and tenderly taking care of those yourself.

I really accept that solid relationships start with the one we have with ourselves. That incorporates assuming full liability for all parts of ourselves and our lives.

Appreciation

When I was amidst the madness of narcissistic maltreatment, I had an inclination that I was in a horrific experience! At the time, I totally could never have engaged the idea of applying appreciation to the experience! Presently, however, numerous years after the fact, I can really say I am profoundly appreciative for the experience.

When I got mindful of this specific sort of mental and psychological mistreatment, the sheer profundities of the agony I was encountering impelled me to set out on a profound voyage of investigation, recuperating, and recuperation and tremendous self-improvement, which I am presently unceasingly appreciative for.

I effectively working on expounding on what I could be appreciative for in each piece of the experience and—as difficult as that was at the time—it helped my mending.

I found out about narcissistic maltreatment, I figured out how to recognize the indications of both unmistakable and secretive narcissism so now I can detect this a mile off. With mindfulness, I have a decision.

I needed to investigate my part in the dynamic, my issues of codependency. I learned limits. I've learned sound correspondence. I worked with a specialist and care group to feel and recuperate the family causes of certain issues that identified with why we pull in or rehash undesirable relationship designs in any case.

I figured out how to tune into and confide in myself and my gut nature; I generally remain near that now. I took in a colossal sum about myself. I comprehend what solid relationships are and appreciate a significant number of them in my life now. I'm a superior, more astute, and progressively thankful individual for experiencing everything.

Try not to misunderstand me, I could never need to encounter it until kingdom come! In any case, I rest certain now that, because of a full recuperation, I totally will never need to. I don't draw in that sort of individual any longer. Truth be told, I can be a remarkable narcissist-repellant because I perceive the admonition signs. Just as detecting the signs outwardly and perceiving the damaging activities of others, I presently have clear limits and the confidence to convey them.

I have likewise chipped away at what should have been mended within me, and for that I am thankful.

Working The 5 Phases of Trauma Recovery After Narcissistic Abuse

When individuals consider injury, they will in general envision separated occasions like cataclysmic events or fender benders.

Yet, injury can take numerous structures.

Narcissistic maltreatment is a spirit squashing type of injury because it gradually develops like a torrential slide. As a rule, it influences your personality and psychological wellness on an exceptionally profound level for quite a while.

That is the reason the phases of recuperating after narcissistic maltreatment are a continuous procedure – not a quick occasion.

Recuperating from complex injury and PTSD from narcissistic maltreatment requires a very different methodology than recouping from disconnected horrible accidents.

Much the same as somebody working through medication or liquor recuperation, it's vital to work through the periods of injury recuperation.

It's not quick or simple, however you'll turn out the opposite end progressively dignified, more grounded, and kinder than you ever were before the maltreatment.

Why Healing from Narcissistic Abuse Is Different

In actuality, complex injury from narcissistic maltreatment is like living under attack from war (battling and mental torment) and a bar (passionate, profound, and even physical disengagement) for a long time.

This isn't to say narcissistic maltreatment is keeping pace with living in a combat area yet that the equivalent mental ramifications are having an effect on everything.

Like somebody living under the danger of war for quite a while, you begin to ask why this maltreatment transpires while others get the opportunity to live in harmony. It feels like you're being tormented by a bar confining your entrance to the remainder of the world.

Without a doubt, something must not be right with you or this maltreatment wouldn't proceed.

This viewpoint for the most part doesn't make a difference in instances of injury from fender benders and other separated occasions.

Indeed, a few people may endure a fender bender and miracle why God would enable a wonder such as this to transpire. However, when all is said in done, individuals will in general perceive that fender benders and cataclysmic events are arbitrary occasions over which they have no control.

Individuals don't typically reprimand themselves for flames and tremors yet we censure ourselves for narcissistic maltreatment. Recuperating from narcissistic maltreatment is different because it assaults your very feeling of self, your mind, and your soul.

How Narcissistic Abuse Affects You on a Deeper Level

Narcissistic maltreatment is a successive result of attempting to have a solid, utilitarian relationship with a character scattered individual over quite a while. It's a disarranged individual's response to having a cozy relationship.

Throughout a relationship with a narcissist, you will create subjective cacophony and an overwhelming injury security because of their key utilization of mental control procedures, for example, the quiet treatment.

From the outset, you may endure a warmed battle once in a while. Things quiet down and you discount it as a one-time occasion.

You disregard the warnings. They're only a tormented soul, correct?

Be that as it may, then the battling builds its pace. You begin to see that in each situation, you're off-base – in any event, when you began the discussion by requesting an expression of remorse or essential regard.

How often have you attempted to go up against the narcissist – even amiably – about something they've done that harmed you just to have them transform the discussion into a harsh circumstance? How frequently have you wound up saying 'sorry' to the narcissist toward the finish of these discussions?

The narcissist should consistently be the person in question – in any event, when they've treated you horrendously.

If the narcissist consistently must be the person in question, that implies another person should consistently be the culprit. That's right, that is your job: You're the foe and they're the hero in the speculative motion picture playing inside the narcissist's head.

The issue is that after weeks, months, or long periods of this extremely unobtrusive control, you start to really trust it on a profound level – for the most part without acknowledging it.

It impacts how you see yourself and everybody around you. You begin to accept that you're useless, can't do anything right, and nobody would ever appreciate your conversation.

The Choice Point

Each time you experience another cycle of psychological mistreatment with the narcissist, there is a fateful opening called a Choice Point. It's in this spot where we get the opportunity to change the negative cycles that have become an example in our lives.

In that space, we can either continue settling on similar decisions that keep us caught in lethal relationships, or we can pick a different way. We can pick different methods for carrying on and different perspectives.

Each decision we make is making our future.

It's trying to stop and consider this when you're in steady battle or-flight mode during narcissistic maltreatment. In any case, the decisions we make now influence our future, yet the fates of our kids, our grandkids, our work environments, our neighborhoods, and our general public.

In snapshots of disloyalty and passionate decimation – which are inevitable inside narcissistic maltreatment – we simply need to rest easy thinking about ourselves, to stop the torment, and for things to change back to "ordinary".

In any case, what we commonly don't consider in those minutes is the thing that could occur in the following week, year, or decade when we decide to remain in poisonous relationships. We don't perceive that we are making swells that will influence our loved ones, others, and eventually, the world.

Numerous individuals accept they're safe from the impacts of narcissistic maltreatment – until they land terminated from their position, their pet is hurt or slaughtered, they have an insane breakdown, or their youngster ends it all because of consistent obnoxious attacks and being made to feel contemptible.

We don't contemplate that we may be demolishing our vocation because we won't quit noting an oppressive accomplice's instant messages in a corporate gathering – putting ourselves in danger of vagrancy.

We may not perceive that when we experience rehashed worry from enthusiastic and obnoxious attack, our minds are being rebuilt... for the more awful.

We don't consider how remaining in harmful relationships will probably set our kids up to be either narcissistic or mutually dependent, accordingly propagating generational brokenness.

Be that as it may, what would you be able to do when you've quite recently discovered the narcissist has cheated (again) or you've found they disclosed to you a whopper of an untruth (again) and everything you can do to traverse the minute is inhale into a paper sack to keep yourself from hyperventilating? What would you be able to do to get off the insane, frequenting thrill ride?

You generally have a decision

It's practically difficult to think sanely during snapshots of psychological mistreatment.

Be that as it may, in any event, during times of insufferable anguish, there exists that part of a second when your psychological personality says, "See, we realized this would occur. I don't have the foggiest idea why you won't hear me out."

Be that as it may, then, your damaged subliminal personality attempts to beat your intellectual personality to the ground. Instantly, you start considering how you can make the narcissist responsible or how you can get once more into their great graces so they'll pick you over their issue accomplice.

These are your decision point occasions. What's more, there are a lot bigger powers having an effect on everything. Decision focuses are not irregular scenes, yet wake up calls. Times where we have to peruse the signs and settle on better decisions.

Some decision focuses are critical in our lives... life-changing defining moments. When we can carry our attention to when significant decision focuses are within reach, our lives can turn out to be enormously improved with far more shrewd decisions.

Narcissistic Abuse Recovery Is a Marathon, Not a Sprint

Complex injury from narcissistic maltreatment sets aside a long effort to create – now and then years or even decades. It's unwise, then, to accept that recuperating from narcissistic maltreatment can be immediate (and you shouldn't confide in any individual who discloses to you generally).

The narcissist went through years gradually working on your feeling of self and soul. Therefore, mending from complex injury and PTSD ought to be a continuous procedure.

Frankly, complete opportunity from the past isn't generally a feasible (or even a perfect) objective.

This is the thing that individuals acknowledge as they work through the periods of injury recuperation.

Narcissistic maltreatment doesn't need to (and shouldn't) be your entire story, yet it is a significant section in your book. It's indiscreet, and truth be told unfortunate, to imagine that you can essentially "snap out" of this attitude while recuperating from narcissistic maltreatment.

Mending from complex injury and PTSD just doesn't work that way. Furthermore, if it did, it would be a ghastly type of otherworldly bypassing.

It's vital to work through the periods of injury recuperation.

The impacts of complex injury from narcissistic maltreatment will tail you wherever you go: as you look for new openings, search for new companions, reconstruct lost relationships, and attempt to build up a character once more.

What's more, that new personality? It will never be the equivalent. It will be more grounded, progressively self-assured, and much more sympathetic than it was before your sincerely harsh relationship.

Mending from narcissistic maltreatment is a difficult and persistent procedure yet it improves.

The Phases of Trauma Recovery

You're presumably effectively acquainted with the five phases of misery. Be that as it may, what is misery? It is a horrendous mishap that influences you on an otherworldly level.

The phases of mending after narcissistic maltreatment are fundamentally the same as. In all honesty, the five phases of despondency are something beyond a plot idea for parody appears. It's critical to work through every one of these phases with an open heart and emotionally supportive network.

Nobody ever expects individuals experiencing substance maltreatment to recuperate medium-term, isn't that so? No, they work through the 12 stages (or other solid recuperation programs). Ask anybody in medication, liquor, or betting recuperation and they'll reveal to you it's a progressing procedure that proceeds with consistently, now and again inconclusively.

This may sound overwhelming, yet have you at any point met somebody with long stretches of strong recuperation? They're versatile, in charge of their feelings, and carrying on with their best life.

It shows signs of improvement. What's more, the five periods of injury recuperation can help. The following, I'm going to walk you through the phases of mending after narcissistic maltreatment, bit by bit, with connections to every one of the assets you need. How about we bounce in...

1. Crisis Stabilization Phase

This first period of narcissistic maltreatment recuperation is the most significant, but at the same time it's the hardest.

You at long last go No Contact from the narcissist and aren't sure if you've settled on the correct choice. (Possibly the police even settled on the choice for you.)

You're still overstimulated from the narcissistic maltreatment which may at present be streaming as writings from odd numbers or transferred messages from shared companions.

What you need right currently is backing and consolation. The injury has felt "typical" for such a long time that encountering security and serenity feels remote and exceptionally off-base. You're as yet powerless and scared of how the narcissist will react to all that you think or do.

During the Emergency Stabilization Phase, it's basic to keep in touch or, on account of shared guardianship, Extreme Modified Contact.

If you do impart authority to the narcissist, it's basic to acknowledge that being respectful and developed isn't a piece of the narcissist's cosmetics. Therefore, don't subside into an incorrect feeling that all is well with the world when the narcissist guarantees you they will come through for the children or be straightforward with you going ahead.

When you are bamboozled by their stunts and ulterior thought processes, they consider it to be an encouragement to continue exploiting you… and to proceed with their oppression and autocracy over your life.

The Emergency Stabilization Phase is commonly the most difficult to suffer because of the clairvoyant destroy to reconnect with the narcissist and the biochemical compulsion that creates subsequent to suffering rehashed injuries. Breaking No Contact is without a doubt the main explanation individuals remain ensnared in lethal relationships any longer than they expect to, which is the reason keeping in touch ought to be your top need during the phases of mending after narcissistic maltreatment.

2. Punching Upwards Phase

This is when you begin to lift yourself back up off the floor. Your vitality begins to return after the narcissist depleted it for such a long time. (Being the objective of narcissistic maltreatment requires a ton of your time and consideration.)

You may encounter floods of outrage towards the narcissist and even at yourself for enabling the maltreatment to continue for such a long time. Without legitimate help and recuperation, you may slip over into stage one. It's critical to take note of that while bolster bunches on open online networking destinations may help in the first place, they are not a wellspring of legitimate help and can eventually hinder you in your recuperation.

Numerous individuals don't understand that the explanation they feel so unreliable and edgy in the wake of going No Contact is that they have an uncertain connection style, which manifests as open, crude passionate injuring, just as devastating sentiments of deserting and dismissal in the wake of narcissistic maltreatment.

Regardless of whether your connection style wasn't to a great extent uncertain in the start of your poisonous relationship, it is absolutely that path after narcissistic maltreatment.

Individuals with shaky connection styles center eagerly around keeping the narcissist close, to the detriment of their own advantages and even their very own qualities. This somewhat clarifies why narcissistic maltreatment unfortunate casualties fold under requests, for example, over and again sympathetic acts of unfaithfulness or consenting to work and cover every one of the tabs while the narcissist skips and plays with their other stockpile sources.

This happens because they're urgently attempting to connect to the narcissist, which just prompts more sentiments of basic frenzy. The best way to balance this inclination is to discover a genuinely accessible connection figure in the wake of starting No Contact. This may be a companion, relative, specialist, mentor, or God – at the end of the day, somebody who can be your Rock of Gibraltar... at any rate during the underlying months of No Contact.

This is the place a proven narcissistic maltreatment recuperation program can have a significant effect.

3. One Foot in the Door Phase

The third of the key phases of recuperating after narcissistic maltreatment is fragile. You begin to remake your character, yet your past will in general disrupt everything. You may begin to give the narcissist an excess of credit and think "we both treated each other inadequately" or "they've encountered misuse, as well."

In spite of the fact that it's less basic than during stage two, you can return to the previous periods of injury recuperation whenever absent much by way of caution. That is the reason backing and direction from experienced experts or transformational mentors are so significant during the whole procedure.

Since you're beginning to feel positive about yourself and your choices, you may feel constrained to connect with the narcissist on easygoing terms. Perhaps they've changed? (They haven't.)

During this stage, you will manage withdrawal from the biochemical dependence that shaped after rehashed cycles of misuse. When you're in withdrawal, your mind will reveal to all of you sorts of things to get you to reach so you can get a surge of dopamine. It will disclose to you that things can return to the manner in which they used to be, before the maltreatment set in with full power.

For a brief period, this thought will appear to be attainable as your mind sticks onto delicate recollections, leaving you with a throbbing long. You'll persuade yourself you overcompensated to everything. In any event, you'll end up looking for conclusion or a clarification. Be that as it may, notice, connecting with the narcissist will slow down you in your recuperation, or more awful, land you straight go into the cycle of misuse.

Simply solicit survivors from narcissistic maltreatment who attempted this methodology.

4. Target Analysis Phase

Now in recuperating from narcissistic maltreatment, you can glance back at your past unbiasedly without feeling overpowered with feelings like indignation or a lot of disappointment.

You've invested a lot of energy looking inwards and identifying enthusiastic triggers left over from the narcissistic maltreatment. Presently, you're prepared to begin helping other people who are in the early periods of injury recuperation.

Despite the fact that you've placed a great deal of work into remaking your personality, you may wind up slipping go into sentiments of uselessness or questioning your capacity. You probably won't understand this is a hold-over from the maltreatment, yet it is.

This is the place most narcissistic maltreatment survivors experience the ill effects of the manifestations of endeavored perspecticide.

Evan Stark, an honor winning scientist and teacher at Rutgers is credited as first begetting the expression "perspecticide" in his 2007 book, Coercive Control. Perspecticide is the insufficiency to realize what you know, because of misuse.

With perspecticide, the abuser gradually works on your viewpoint until you have no musings of your own. Perspecticide was first utilized as a mental control strategy on detainees of war and later by clique pioneers, points I've expounded on previously.

The objective is to accomplish an all-out loss of character in the proposed target.

All things considered, it's a lot simpler to control an individual when they have no contemplations, sentiments, and sentiments of their own.

When you end up slipping go into the shadows of loss of self, recollect how far you've come. You never again must be influenced by the narcissist's verbal holocaust or rude feelings. You never again must be their passionate punching sack or container for their contempt.

If you've found a way to free yourself, your life is a fresh start on which you can paint a beautiful watercolor of your future.

5. Acknowledgment and Reintegration Phase

You can see things obviously and as they may be. You know your capacities and restrictions – not the ones the narcissist railed into you.

Now, you see how to create solid relationships and you have the boldness to make a move if somebody attempts to treat you inadequately.

Absolutely never let your gatekeeper down something over the top however – narcissists are all over the place. Be that as it may, you've figured out how to confront their maltreatment before it gets excessively far.

Mending from Complex Trauma and PTSD from Narcissistic Abuse

It's totally significant to travel through the five periods of injury recuperation as you're mending from narcissistic maltreatment. You have to investigate how the injury created so as to disentangle it for good.

Be that as it may, with the correct help, you can – and you'll be stunned how astonishing it feels when you can thrive on the opposite side.

Lightning Source UK Ltd.
Milton Keynes UK
UKHW022035280521
384576UK00002B/285